I0763108

BLACK MOUNTAIN

CHAMBERLAIN

BLACK MOUNTAIN

CHAMBERLAIN

John Chamberlain's Writings at Black Mountain College, 1955

Edited by Julie Sylvester

Distributed by Princeton University Press, Princeton and Oxford

BLOND DAY

The only time I ever became interested in anyone or where I became interesting to anyone else was when I went to Black Mountain College. Black Mountain was introduced to me by Gerry van de Wiele, a friend of mine from Chicago. It was a nice place, very country, mountainy, just east of Asheville, North Carolina, Tom Wolfe's old home. Joel Oppenheimer was there, Stefan Wolpe was there, I took a little music course with him. Charles Olson was there, Robert Duncan was there, Robert Creeley came there for a while, a guy named Wes Huss who was interested in theater....actually Wes liked to sit around and watch everything else go on as though it were theater. Joseph Fiore, Dan Rice and Tom Field were artists there. People had their families, there were about five students and fifteen teachers. It was 1955, kind of the final year of Black Mountain College. The school sort of dribbled down from there. The attitude of the people who went there was that of graduate students, interested in the information and the knowledge that they were acquiring, and having to deal with it on a daily basis. You could start anywhere at any time. You could take everything or you could take nothing. There were work schedules that were funny but never lasted. Black Mountain had its life. It went through a lot of different changes, a lot of different regimes. Its most crowded was when it had ninety students.

At Black Mountain College, everyone was reading books. You had to read about the Old West, you had to read anything D.H. Lawrence wrote, and Ezra Pound and William Carlos Williams, and detective stories by Dashiell Hammett and Raymond Chandler. All of those areas were very popular. I would read and when I'd see a word I liked, I'd isolate it, I'd write it down. So I had this collection of words I liked to look at. It didn't matter what they meant, I liked the way they looked. So I would look at the words, and I would put the words together and I would come up with an image that was unlike anything you would perceive if you didn't do it this way. I remember one line I wrote where I put together two words: *blond day.* I'd never thought of a day being blond. I still haven't, but I liked the way that the connection went together, and it's a very good example of how I feel I work. I still go around and process stuff in the same way. There is material to be seen around you every day. But one day something, some one thing, pops out at you and you pick it up and you take it over and you put it somewhere else and it fits, and it's just the right thing at the right moment. It's actually doing things in the same way, with words or with metal.

I guess that's part of my definition of art. Art is a particular madness where you are using a means of communication, which means are recognizable to other people, to say something that they hadn't heard, or hadn't perceived, or had repressed. Curiously, it's only recently that I've noticed that I'm still making sculptures in the way that I made the poems. *It's all in the fit.* Say you take one word that's on a page. You like this word, this word looks nice to you. Maybe you don't even care what the word means. But you like the word. You can conjugate the word. If the word is beauty, it can become beautiful. Then it can become beauteous, can't it? Or beautification. You can play around with it, add to it, or if you want you can take the word apart. You can play with the letters in the word, that's making anagrams. There's also a way of taking the syllables apart, rearranging the syllables.

What I do is not unlike this. In quite a few of these stories I am telling you, I didn't get their point until years later.

When I went to Black Mountain, I found that there were other people who spoke with tension, trying to find out what they didn't know. Everybody else before them had been happy with what they knew. They weren't curious about what they didn't know. Probably the main description of the occupation of art is to find out what you don't know. By starting someplace that's curious and delving in, in a common way, and coming out with an uncommon satisfaction, an uncommon piece of knowledge, that is very satisfying to your nervous system.

The greatest influence on my work and on my thinking actually came from the poets at Black Mountain College. As far as the poetry I wrote then, I'm certain it was all very personal. There isn't a body of work, so I couldn't include myself as a poet in the poet sense, like Creeley is. See, Creeley, is a real poet. Whether it's on a postcard or the way he phrases sentences, he works with words. He has his own manners and attitudes in that regard. He understands my foam sculpture, but that doesn't make him a sculptor. From having the foam sculpture around, did he understand the wadding technique, or the compression? Not necessarily. But the next time he washed the dishes, when he squeezed the sponge and one end of it popped out of the end of his fist, it looked like the sculpture. It was because of the one that he could see the other. He could get an added perception. It's daily life. That's where I get the idea that everybody makes sculpture every day, whether in the way they wad this up or the way they throw the towel over the rack or the way they wad up the toilet paper. That's all very personal and very exact, and in some sense very skillful on their part, but it is discarded as not-useful information. But it's not not-useful. These little things, like blowing up the paper bag and hitting it so it pops – say you take it one little step further and you do it in slow motion and you explore what resistance of the air in the bag is, and you make something. That is to me very interesting. If there is a body of work demonstrating all these things that come together, that's useful in art history, as part of the accumulation of how knowledge goes on and on and on in this particular occupation.

The few sculptures that I made at Black Mountain were strongly influenced by David Smith. The first piece of David Smith's that I saw was *Agricola Nine*, it was at the Art Institute of Chicago. I liked it a lot because it wasn't representing something else, or it didn't seem so to me, and it was a very strange looking thing, and I sort of liked it because it was strange and I hadn't seen anything like that before. It was nice to be around. The pieces *Clytie* and *Calliope*, *Clytie* especially, look similar to it. In the development of both of those pieces, I found myself working in that area, I was trying to put the top part of *Clytie* in the other one, but when I put it in the right place, it connected up in three different places, so it told me how to put it together. I think in this particular area, in the way I've gone about this, I've led a charmed life. David Smith was quite good, I felt, but as I got to know him more and more, the pieces got smaller to me, and then I started disagreeing with his attitude about a lot of things, and then I thought he was very flat, but I still liked him a lot, besides, he looked like my father and we were born about sixty miles apart. He came from In Diana also.

John Chamberlain
From interviews conducted by Julie Sylvester
in Sarasota and New York, 1981–1984

1

INTAGLIO

i saw ~~once~~ that a
cloud of ink was pass-
ing my door, birds with
bloated bodies squirted
squid-like gall from the
eave; the soybeans ~~were~~
that grew in the field
lay rotting in the shale
that no longer was able
to hold weeds. i wanted
so much to ~~hold~~ TAKE the wings
& fly away, no; "stand there
and behave, you little shit."
linger longer under the pear
tree with me, across the
roof to my hideout, our nest.
there was no choice, i carved
my initals on her stomach
with my teeth, my
first sculpture.

i saw her
WALK GENTLY ~~WITH~~
with brown against
OFAY
blond day
HANGING LIKE fusing
~~fusing~~ breasts,
AZALEAS
above a neckline a.
LA CABEZA
sloped into
A CRADLE, ~~THAT~~ Rocked ~~into~~ a
valley of desire
FITS TIGHTLY
like silk sheets
WRAPPED
around ~~next to~~ a nude, velvet
~~AUGUST~~ RIPENED
marijuana sister
FLAT-BELLIED
from shanty town
SINGING WILDLY
hush crazy baby
LAY DOWN YR
cheap cotton dresses
& RUN,RUN,RUN,
in the sun.

this is the cradle
and the cradle is the grave
rocked by the hand, the hand
spits forcibly

a violet in the rain
~~being-picked~~ a thigh as snow
~~on~~ pure intoxication

the locus is here
belly flat against the
object

a violet in the rain
a thigh as snow
pure intoxication
the locus is here
belly flat against the

i saw her
brown against ~~a~~
blond day
fusing breasts
above a neckline
sloped into
valley of desire
like silk sheets
next to a nude ~~body~~

marijuana sister
from shanty town
hush crazy baby
cheap cotton dresses
in the sun

walk gently with
ofay
hanging like
azaleas
la cabeza
a cradle, that
fits tightly
wrapped
august ripened

flat bellied
singing wildly
lay down yr
& run,run,run

i saw her walk gently

with brown against ofay,

blond day hanging like fusing

breasts, ~~[illegible], DAGWOOD [illegible]~~,

above a neckline

la cabeza

sloped into a cradle,

rocked to a ~~valley~~ tune of

~~deire~~ desire fits tightly,

like silk sheets wrapped

around a nude, velvet

ripened marijuana sister,

flat-bellied, ~~from shanty town~~ ~~[illegible]~~

singing ~~wildly~~, SOFTLY

hush crazy baby,

lay down your cheap

cotton dresses &

run, run, run,

in the sun.

i saw her walk gently
with brown against ofay,
blond day hanging like fusing
breasts above a neckline,
la cabeza
sloped into a cradle,
rocked to a tune of
desire, fits tightly
like silk sheets wrapped
around a nude, velvet
ripened marijuana sister,
flat-bellied from shanty town
singing softly,
hush crazy baby
lay down your cheap
cotton dresses &
run,run,run,
in the sun.

the girls in the water
made southern sounds
with their painted like
mayan hierogliphics.

the street giggled at the girls
that giggled southern sounds thru
their faces painted like mayan
hierogliphics, beat a tattoo on
saturday night and the street died
the death of a rag doll; all the
sawdust went to their heads.

the girls in the water
made southern sounds with their
faces painted like mayan hiero-
gliphics, i had to listen~~ed~~ to the
garble of their warble as the
fat one ate ice cream, dripping
down her arm. mountain covered
beach-houses watched the speading
olive oil lay on the white, white
skin, rolling on a towel to the
edge of secluded monotony.
~~the tattooed man wanted to go~~
~~jump in the lake~~

mountain covered beach-houses
watched the speading olive-
oil lay on the white, white
skin, rolling to the edge
of secluded monotony. the girls
in the water made southern
sounds with their faces painted
like mayan hierogliphics. the
tombs opened like a ritual, un-
covering ~~a~~ gilt-edge sex machines
rusting with inactivity, glides
to the waters edge
i listen to their giggles and watch
the one in the brown suit with huge
unused breasts eat an ice cream mostly
running down her arm. juxtaposed are
oh nuts!

i have abbreviated you
to a pimple to be
squeezed between two
thumbnails, and

i have walked on you
with the inportance of
stepping on an ant, what
a squishy thing you were

you have been dehydrated
by the culchur drought
and it'll never rain again
in your time. so

why dont you just go &
get lost.

i asked her for a date, but
she only had a fig, fig it.

she said that she liked apples
so i gave her a pineapple

her eyes thumbed thru the words
of the book like eyes watching
a game of tennis, between her fingers
the cigarette burned to oblivion
as did the words of the words of
the book.

i had a chocolate soda for breakfast
and belched all the way till noon.

the t.v. set had a tongue drawn on the
face of the screen,sticking out, the knobs
had fingers painted over the numbers and
the visitors refused to touch it, we have
finally found a way to casterate jackie
gleason from this house.

the air hangs thick
around the space
on delicate stilts and
follows the words i
pin to the wall. and

some words stick in
a framed atmosphere of
a lead gray background
offering the silloutte
not seen with the eyes.

but dancing in a round
room built to
have its walls pined & pinned,
the thought dropped
and broke my toe. i

am not content to
sit by and hold my
extremities ? etc. nor
flake the dirt with
an unbroken toe.

occuput

(if
i were dead
but as you see i'm close to it
having watched it rattled off with my father
my mother,sister and the rest of that which is
called ones family
(to be sure
they still breath,anattribute of the living.
i here claim it for the dead
i here also claim that -
protected as they are ~~xxxthexx~~
~~xxxxxxfuckxthm~~

(fuck em

on wings of ice a woman with
hot
her eyes quiver
under a sheet of swiftly
moving
pajamas, cool.

i want to write a
poem that fits in
the middle of the
sea, walks on fire
at night in the search
lights that round
a curve of yr hip
swinging in the wind
past a curious eye, i
want to see the night
sound its presence
on a battlefield of
scar tissue not water-
skiing behind a rocket
ship; a lot of hot
air in yr face.

anywhere where the land
grows grass,
our feet should stand
without aid,

the cat lookd at the mouse
was not fast enough to
eat his dinner so i feed her
catfish.

i shot him on a rainy afternoon.
on a dreary day i blew his brains
out.
in & out of the money,

sun

is what is taken by the horns
not the bull

i longto talk to my lover

when rocks glimmer
plants will bough
curtsy in the wind

come lover rest in my
heart while stars fall

in yr hand you
hold the glass of
sand sifting thru
fingers borne
of years gone,

yr beauty lies in
the instant, the
experience to live
full beyond past
the day loaded;

in this hand
pinecones spread
hang from each finger-
tip to the yawning
jaws of lions, at
yr feet.

(full-grown)

yr cymbals crackle
i,
Cybele,
great mother

experience is
in the midst

there were violets & gumdrops
in your hand and they were
changed to cymbals & pinetrees;
you walk now on hot concrete
embellished head of golden crown.

in the midst of a wind
that knocks a few heads
together like the sounds
of croquet, my ice cream
cone was demolished between
my teeth.

the monster in rm 12

ti me for bre ak fas t in the innersanctum.

love own n sweet song @ 20¢ a pound.

the dance of the fireflys

last night i tied the moon
to the sky to light
my way a rocky road, in a
clearing to the left not un-
lit a daisy nodded
thank you, for letting me
show myself and i myself
shown back in the light i
tied with a slipknot that
slipped around a half round
moon.

super market

in this cage of inertia
breaking their backs over
canned ham vacuum-packed
morons conscienciously put
pickles on a shelf.

shoving cans to the right
bottles to the left

a white square over
a wooden horse
the afternoon sun streams
in thru a window at the left across a book p opened
and blankets a pretty maiden
sitting near a round table holding a cigarette
an arm across her breast scratching a bite on her other arm
a white blouse, short sleeved & opened necked
tucked neatly into a flowered skirt
an ear lobe filled with pearl

the girl was

promoting most of her

way coming to her, to say she

made the most of , wd

simply t act

pleasure borne in mind, she

broke herself in two

parts; it kept her enjoying

herself.

i am free now, to
practice as i please, as
i see it,
laying in my bed
to much, things
dont get
done like
they should
of.

bfgryux igu
d tones, you open
[illegible]

on mountain covered beach
houses, lonely strechs of
golden strings attached to
fingers, connected & arms
length to the day, growing
old, growing back to child-
hood, black dawns fill the
gray skies seeping thru the
cracks of the old house. &
there the frame carries the
rag doll, by the foot. groan
is the bone that's rubbed
against the pain of barbed
wire that keeps you in. counting
squares with the fish, fisheye;
the day has been carried,
so come on now,
drop it.

ode to fenollosa

(if
i were bill williams
i'd write about that white horse
in that green field (chewing grass

(that is -
i xxx
see
a
man
see
a
horse

(i saw a horse
in a manyplies green field
eating grass.

JUN 25 55

everything is,so far,ok. not in the least wise gragglepaged

hoever on the face of things the squimert just might come in 1st

the rain crushed the
earth and clouds shrank
from the relief, belief
felt muddy by the constant
sunless image thru a
window, the nakedness
tacked to a wall, says
" the clarinet plays the
blues while strolling
thru the ghost town streets",
lights not lit, littered
occupants, and below the sea
the vegetables grow just as
green as green is. green
jungle beats a rythum on
the tattooed man chest and
bellows the same old hot air
that has been keeping the fires
from going out plus the rain
and the fog and the things that
are and the things that aint.
there in the center of it all
somebody keeps dancing a sorta
tango(maybe for two) like the
slow agony of the waltz thats
done when man gets shot in the left
side just below the ribs with a
.22. $\frac{3}{4}$ of $\frac{1}{4}$ equal abt 18$\frac{3}{4}$ if you
happen to be thinking abt twenty-
five ¢ pieces. and @ two for a $
the exchange rate is even higher in
the west.

~~we took a banana &~~
~~called it cubism, it~~
~~was peeled by lipchitz~~
~~giocemetti ate it with salt~~
~~smith used the skin to~~
~~make agricula,~~
i'm making a new banana.
gaudier tells how the friut
developed, in a tree, in a sphere,
always to a point. a vortex.
the greeks played ball with the
sphere, against the wall like a
firing squad. wanderings across the
frieze you call it. flat, flat.
fat myron rounded the ball again
& threw it to rome, they put their
heads in it, space-men then.
the indians over east really knew
what side to chisel on, emotion,
black mystery, sez they. all this
time the vortex is being made, in the
sphere, elongated by hthe africans

and hit on the head by pablo
to cube it, disarrange the planes
for better or worse, the bauhaus
found the bananas upside down &
left them. lipchitz peeled the thing
for the next ten years, only to have
giocemetti eat it, with salt yet.
damn if smith didn't start welding the
peel back together again. nothing's
happening now jim, the contemparies
are still buzzing around like a bunch
of lost bees, lost in the top of the
vortises. ~~t its quite simple to take~~
~~the sphere~~
we'er back with the sphere again and
as i see it its got to be laid open
bare, bottom of the vortex, begin scaling
those walls again.
i'm making a new banana.

time hangs
like buckleing knees
in snowshoes
the thing i s
who to brace them
brace them unbending
back again.

yielding hamstrings
rounding first
snapping into second.

the turth is
earth slants &
~~plants-~~
seedlings grow at
45 degree angles.

the disremembered lie at night
open eyed
big as saucers,
silence damn drum
let me have one word
alone
beneath the sand,
turning, squirming, burning,
fight bbl-aa-stt it.
SOAKEN sheet

like holding a thicken tongue
cooled between yr lips
like wetted soft folds
like not so mirrored eyes running
like water over the dam;

what fever breaks
without trial?

slitting slot sliping silently

consumption of the bird
flowered weed flowing
~~mirrored eyes running~~
~~water over the dam~~
cooled between yr lips
how little of the friut
is tasted when fences
built solidly around &
about the greedy fingers
of renegade holders,
demanding more.

~~there~~ holding a thicken tongue
cooled between yr lips
~~has not~~ wetted soft folds
~~folded, foundled~~, ~~feeling~~
not so ~~foolish~~, ~~fowl.~~

mirrored eyes running,
like water over the dam,
~~down along patienceless~~
~~ending days.~~

what fever breaks
without trial?

tocutit

to cut off my head
to spite my face
would be shear
suicide.

to my old fried friend: jogoto

this is a poem dedicated to a picture that hangs on the wall of my father's tavern.

time hangs
        limply through the noose
        feet dragging the ground
        dangling eyes of spectators
        whipping sharply over the orange
        necked niggers
        hell bent for heaven.

0-0-0-0-0-0-0-0-0-0-0-0-0-0-0-0-0

like holding a thicken tongue,
like wetted soft folds,
like not so mirrorēd eyes running,
like water over the dam
        cooled between your lips
                what fever breaks
                                without trial?

0-0-0-0-0-0-0-0-0-0-0-0-0-0-0-0-0

when afternoon's rain
 falls as your kisses off
  my eyes, my hand touches tender
   beauty beneath your ear,
    grasp me sweetly with ivory fingertips
     my Deare, and be anxious no more.

Chamberlain

time hangs
limply through the noose
feet dragging the ground
dangling eyes of spectators
whipping sharply over the orange
necked niggers
hell bent for heaven.

like holding a thicken tongue,
like wetted soft folds,
like not so mirrored eyes running,
like water over the dam
cooled between your lips,
what fever breaks
without trial?

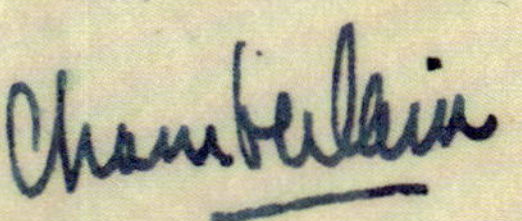

in morning light that chases me abt,
like the hound in my lovers heart,
i curse the days & sleepless nights,
that lie between our chosen part.

~~the-moon-caresses~~

for i had rather owner be
of thee one hour, than all else ever.
(else)

forms that are you
stirring space there
hold a thickened tongue
cooled between yr lips
what fever breaks
broken by trial

when i died last, and i die /
when as often as i am from you, /
i go, /
if only an hour be, /
lovers hours be full /
eternities. /

the difference between u& me
is 800 miles.

i died last, & i die
as often as from you
i go,
if only an hour,
lovers hours be full
eternities.

i had rather
owner of you
one hour, than all
else ever.

i am disarranged
                  not in form
in the contents of
                   my mind, my mind
does not fall
                 among the patterned
landscapes of
                 this construction and
the blow cracks
                  the mass like a
hammer bouncing
                  off an anvil.

on the close of the year i have left
behind my energy;

the times enjoyed with you have come
to an end; remember

those delightful evenings around a
cocktail, cigar

smoke curling in the air about a
finger outstreched.

my energy has fallen beside the chiseled
leavings, leaving little

lumps of scultures standing in memorium
of those battled

days when things were soaked in a bag
of plaster,

plastered on a frame framed to the like-
ness of a

friendship i shall always hold close,
tightly by the

skin on your nose that now is healed
by

to e. c.

on the close of the year i have left
behind my energy;

my energy has fallen besides the chiseled
leavings, leaving little

lumps of sculptures standing in memorium
to these battled

days when things were soaked in a bag of
plaster,

plastered on a frame framed to the like-
ness of a

friendship i shall always hold close
tightly by the

skin on your nose that now is healed
by

those delightful evenings around a
cocktail, cigar

smoke curling in the air about a finger
forgetting

the times enjoyed with you have come to an
end.

i am not content
with the way the
poem is written or
the manner that words
fall on the paper.

they are laboured
under a tortured
finger pressing them
out like grapes be-
neath the feet.

the air hangs thick
around the space ~~on~~
ON delicate stilts and
follows the words i
pin to the wall. AND

some words stick fine
in a framed atmosphere
of ~~soft~~ LEAD gray background
offering the silloutte
not seen with the eyes.

but later, dancing, in
a round room built to
have its walls pined &
pinned the thought dropped
and broke my toe. i

am not content to
sit by and hold my
extremities ? etc.
nor flake the dirt
with an unbroken toe.

the crow cocks a slingshot
~~the street paved with rain~~
in the east the sun comes/thru clouds
~~[illegible]~~ pellets clatter
the buildings are orange &
the street is paved with rain.

doorways catapult men into fields
of smokeing beer bottles,
running on suction cups past
glass eyes ~~[illegible]~~ closed with dignity
the street is paved with rain.

the trains run into the ~~[illegible]~~
ear.
clocks pour coffee; automatic apperatus
pops-up capsuled toothpicks, guides
bodys into the maze ~~[illegible]~~
of hairpins
the street is paved with rain.

the crow cocks a slingshot
the buildings are orange
in the east the sun comes thru the clouds
the street is paved with rain.

the trains run into the ear
clocks pour coffee; beds pop-up
like frozen milk, muscles like steve's
e string; broken into a maze of hairpins.

doorways catapult men into fields
of smoking dogwood leaves,
running high on suction cups
past glass eyes closed with dignity.

stand

stand close to me and talk
slowly every word must sing
sing in the pulse that meters
the beat of our love

stand close to me and talk
talk of the lonelyness that
detaches so sublimely the
air of their world

stand close to me and talk
whisper the delight of your
soul when evening comes
& cloaks you & i

foultips off my nose
burned fingers underfed
life in an instant
is the way you say it
saddle up cyrano &
let's go.

in a glimse
her eyes carried ~~to~~
~~me~~ on long legs, sort
of a lanky, angular
strides that gave a
casual shiftless NOD
~~who gives a shit?~~

on the other hand
offered on a plate of
worms crawling over
the edge gulping the
hook, off to a fish
dinner.

in the middle of the
floor came the legs
flashing up the sides
to a garter of flaming
azaleas, wilted by the
chafing.

beneath the BERRY TREE

a wedding

anticipation rose along the wall
of experience that stood as a
monument of their desire, a need
developed in their bio functions
to create a place--
a place to make themselves measured
assurded to an action--
in pagan dress,
standing afront the diety, GOD,
affirms the cross borne of decision

the gallery is filled
with voices singing,
badly, gregorian chant
out of the side of their
mouths. the lamb is placed

upon a disk a disk placed
gently on the tongue,
forced in every vein,
to the end the vows are
echoed thru plastered

of men sitting

the farmers game broke
my back, went numb from
thought of sweating, pulling
a teat when at the store
you can buy it @
half the price.

that idea flew by and
good it did fly, the
tree bent in the wind, crack,
down across a creek

flowers in the garden
a flower garden between the
weeds, grew the damnest
poppy you ever did see
between the eyes, left you
beathing in big gulps of
pure acting on a stage
built of balsa wood and
nailed together with scotch
tape(a la bishop) busted
under the weight of ten lead
men looking for a hand-out.
forty-five fingers were in the
pie and no plums. plumes hung
on the hat and pins pinched
the scalp between the hairs
reached security. sitting in a
rose room full of roses reeking
garlic. and little charlie brown
came by to wish us all the
worst there was.

i am disarranged

not in form

in the contents of my mind, my mind

~~does not~~

forward to be counted, by the numbers,

with the index finger. (cadium red tipped)

i was never there maybe i

forgot

not where but how to sharpen the

razor on a strop

strap behind the curtains of the fleecians

dull ~~nt~~ sharpless

chiseltop

flattened out

for C.O.

the afternoon had sun you
felt on the back of yr head leaning
forward, between halves, no
band, silent; save
the look across the green to
me.   i say nerves
nervey
of me but from you i
see a kindness
that becomes you.

nuts to John Chamberlain

of rocks
of feathers
where shall you go?

you are an acorn
to me the seed that
see's forty feet over
the ground you drop
me to.
----------6-6-6-6-6

the negros stroll offbeat
in the park, near a tree
a man belchs bending green
flame on the head of a dog.

two squirrels gather people
standing ~~in xxbwxwxhx~~
on a rose bush feeding
lemons to the sparrows.

i could not
see what the po-
liceman was
saying to the fellows in the water, but
pointed to a
sign saying:
"thin ice"

A Sound

in the night is quiet
as the dawn is orange

in the yellow tree near
a window of blue, a hum

threatens one eardrum
with rank resonense, a

pulling down, a root, an
anchor, followed by a moan

of life waking in sleepful
restlessness, turning the

clock to see a face, any
face. not so alone in

the ride without gravity
down the hum goes too, along

my ear, spreads over the
eyes of the face, the face

startles at the minute of
reality of the sound stopped.

The poems written by John Chamberlain at Black Mountain were given to Julie Sylvester by Chamberlain in the early 1980s. A selection was made for this publication and is reproduced in facsimile. Chamberlain's spirit remains in his words, one imagines the sound of his big fingers pounding the typewriter keys.

Julie Sylvester is a curator and the author of *John Chamberlain: A Catalogue Raisonné of the Sculpture 1954–1985*. She is the former Associate Curator of Contemporary Art at the State Hermitage Museum, St. Petersburg, Russia, where she curated the first contemporary exhibitions in the institution's history: Louise Bourgeois, Cy Twombly and Willem de Kooning. Her concentration in the past years has been on exhibitions and writings on Cy Twombly.

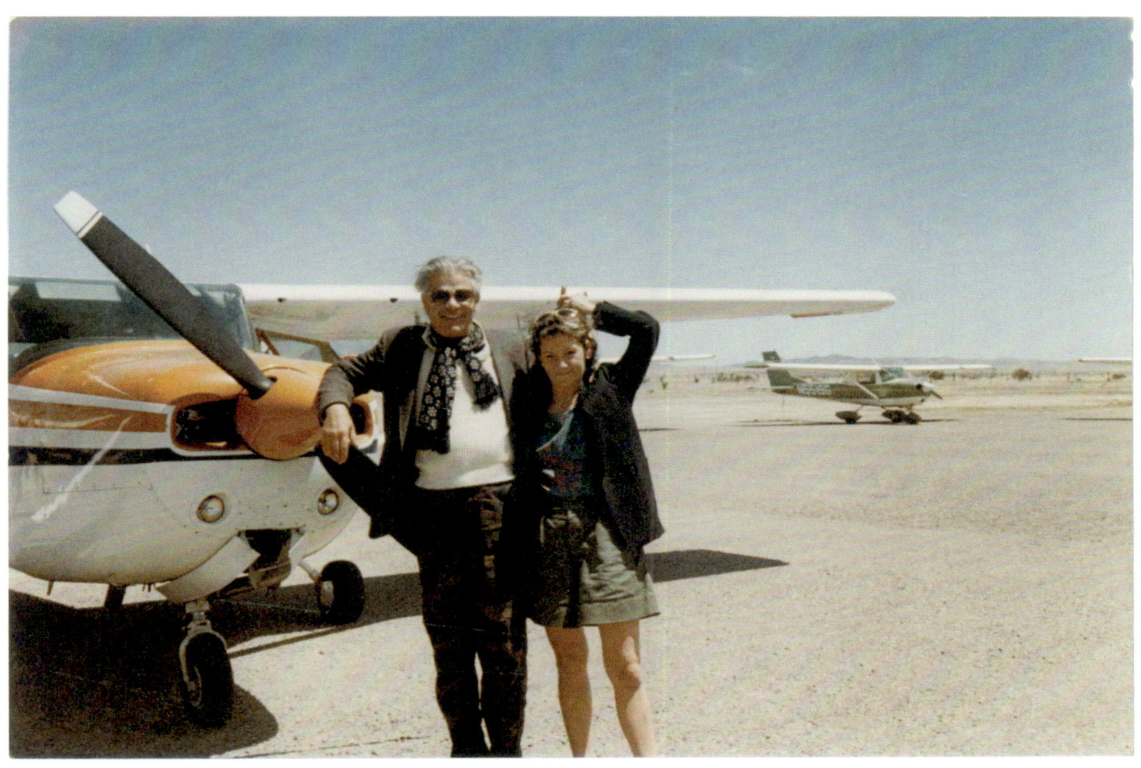

John Chamberlain and Julie Sylvester, Marfa, Texas, 1984

St. George, Bermuda
juliesylvester@northrock.bm

Distributed by Princeton University Press
41 William Street, Princeton, New Jersey 08540
6 Oxford Street, Woodstock, Oxfordshire OX20 1TR
press.princeton.edu

Black Mountain Chamberlain
John Chamberlain's Writings at Black Mountain College, 1955
Edited by Julie Sylvester

ISBN 978-0-691-20448-2
Library of Congress Control Number 2019952273
British Library Cataloging-in-Publication Data is available

Design: Hans Werner Holzwarth
This book has been composed in Akzidenz-Grotesk
Printed on acid-free paper
Printed in Italy by Musumeci

Drawing of Clytie, c.1981–84, ink on paper, 12 x 4.5 cm.
Clytie, 1954, is catalogue number 2 in the catalogue raisonné of the sculpture.

10 9 8 7 6 5 4 3 2 1